Pretty in Paper

Crafts for party fun, room decor, and personal style—made by you!

by Aubre Andrus

★ American Girl®

Published by American Girl Publishing
Copyright © 2014 American Girl

Questions or comments? Call 1-800-845-0005,
visit **americangirl.com**, or write to Customer Service,
American Girl, 8400 Fairway Place, Middleton, WI 53562-0497.

Printed in China
14 15 16 17 18 19 20 LEO 10 9 8 7 6 5 4 3 2 1

All American Girl marks are trademarks of American Girl.

Editorial Development: Carrie Anton, Darcie Johnston
Art Direction and Design: Sarah Boecher
Production: Jeannette Bailey, Tami Kepler, Judith Lary, Paula Moon, Kristi Tabrizi
Photography: Bobbi Peterson, Youa Thao
Illustration: Sarah Boecher, Monika Roe
Special thanks to Cupcakes-A-Go-Go

Dear Crafter,

Who knew you could make so much with paper? We did!

With a few snips, a couple of folds, and a dab of glue, you can create your own paper paradise. Card stock, art tissue, and patterned paper can become a rose ring, framed artwork, or pretty hanging poufs—it's your choice!

This book is divided into three parts: accessories, bedroom, and party. Each section is filled with easy-to-follow, illustrated directions for every paper project. We promise you'll want to make each one.

Most of the crafts can be made with paper included with this kit. You can use any paper you like, though, so go ahead and make enough crowns for everyone at the party or folded wallets for your best friends and your sister, too. Also, keep in mind that any craft can be modified. Try using larger-sized paper to make a bigger folded flower (page 40), for example, or smaller-sized paper to make a tiny origami box (page 59).

Happy crafting!

Your friends at American Girl

Craft with Care

Get Help!

When you see this symbol in the book, it means that you need an adult to help you with all or part of the craft. ALWAYS ask for help before continuing.

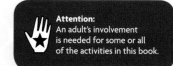

Attention: An adult's involvement is needed for some or all of the activities in this book.

Ask First

If a craft asks you to reuse an item, such as an old shirt or magazine, ask an adult for permission before you use it. Your parent might still need it, so check first.

Craft Smart

Always work on a crafting table or cover your work surface to protect it. If the instruction says *cut,* use safety scissors. If it says *glue,* use craft glue, decoupage glue (Mod Podge®), adhesive dots (Glue Dots®), or a glue stick. If it says *paint,* use a nontoxic acrylic paint. Before using any supplies, ask an adult to look them over—especially paints and glues. Some supplies are not safe for kids.

Put Away Crafts & Supplies

When you're not using the crafts or supplies, put them up high or store them away from little kids and pets.

Paper Crafting Tips

Some of the crafts in this book are more complicated than others. Before you begin, read the directions fully and gather all of the correct supplies. You might want to do the trickier ones with an adult the first time. Here are some additional tips to make your crafts successful:

Paper

Paper refers to thin sheets, and **card stock** refers to thicker sheets. For certain crafts, the exact paper or card stock is named in the supplies list and the sheet itself is labeled.

Glue

Each craft lists the type of glue to use for best results, including adhesive dots, liquid craft glue, a glue stick, and decoupage glue. Use a foam brush, available at craft stores, to apply an even coat of craft glue or decoupage glue.

Folding

To make folds crisp, push the side of a pencil or pen along the crease. Do this for each fold, especially when using card stock.

Cutting

To cut straight lines, use a ruler and a pencil to draw lines on the paper first. To cut circles, trace lids of jars or use a stencil. Always use safety scissors.

Table of Contents

Accessories

Bedroom

Party

Accessories

Express yourself with paper—
no writing required!

Photo Props

Snap some pics with glamorous paper punch-outs.

Supplies

- **Photo Props** card stock
- lollipop stick
- tape
- rhinestone stickers

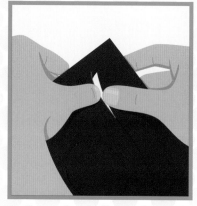

1. Punch out the photo props along the perforated lines.

2. Attach one side of the prop to a lollipop stick with tape.

3. Attach rhinestone stickers to the front for decoration.

Use the photo props as templates, and make mustaches, eyeglasses, hats, and bow ties for your friends. Just trace the template onto card stock from any craft store. Design your own props, too—the options are endless!

Public Library

JH40378812

10 FEDERAL

217955

Folded Wallet

In just 10 folds, your $10 bills can be stylishly stored.

Make a handy pocket for your wallet by cutting a paper rectangle that's slightly smaller than the size of the folded wallet. Fold the right and left sides in ½ inch. Snip the bottom corners; fold the bottom up ½ inch. Line the newly folded side and bottom edges with glue; attach to the inside of the wallet.

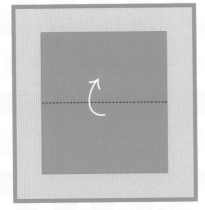

1. Fold wallet paper in half from the bottom to the top. Unfold.

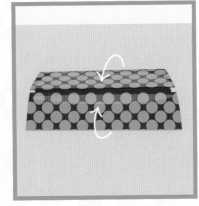

2. Fold the top half down to the center fold. Fold the bottom half up to the center fold.

3. Fold the left and right sides in about 1½ inches.

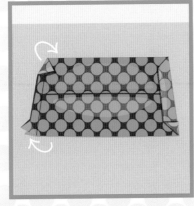

4. On each side flap, fold the bottom corner up toward you to form a small triangle. Then fold the top corners under, away from you, to form small triangles.

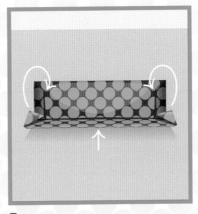

5. Fold the rectangle in half, bottom to top. Tuck the small triangles from the bottom edge into the triangle slots at the top.

6. Fold the rectangle in half, left to right, to complete the wallet.

11

Blooming Barrette

Tissue paper petals bloom with a few snips and folds.

Supplies
- tissue paper
- scissors
- bobby pin

1. Stack six sheets of tissue paper. Cut the stack into a rectangle 4 inches wide by 10 inches long.

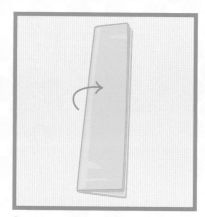

2. Fold the rectangle in half lengthwise so that it's 2 inches wide and 10 inches long.

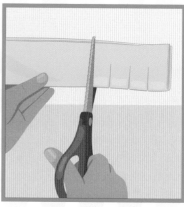

3. Snip slits 1 inch deep along the folded edge to create flower petals.

Use three different shades of paper colors to give the flower dimension.

4. Fold up 1 inch from the end. Keep folding to form a flat roll. Pinch along the bottom edge (not the petal edge) of the flower.

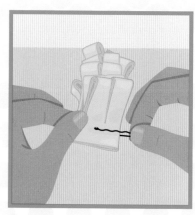

5. Slide the flat flower bottom inside the bobby pin. Gently fluff the petals.

Quilling Shapes

Use your imagination to decorate with delicate paper curls.

Curling thin strips of paper for cool crafts is called *quilling*. Long ago, people used quill feathers to roll the paper—hence the name—but you can use the quilling tool in this kit to make the shapes and crafts shown here.

Tight coils and loose curls

For any shape, start by inserting a strip of quilling paper into the slot in the quilling tool. Roll the strip around the tool; then remove the curled paper from the tool. To adjust the size of the roll for any craft, let it uncoil slightly in your fingers until it's the size you want. Tighter curls will make smaller shapes, and looser curls will make bigger shapes.

Make two-color or three-color coils. Just glue the end of one color strip to the end of another color. Let dry; then curl.

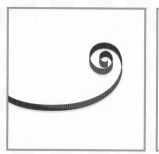

Tight

Loose

Gluing

Secure the curled shape by gluing the end of the paper down with a dab of glue. Squeeze a small amount of craft glue onto a paper plate. Then dip a toothpick into the glue, and place a small drop on the paper. Pinch the glued paper together and hold for several seconds.

Loose spiral

Roll a strip of quilling paper tightly around the quilling tool; then remove the circle from the tool. Let the circle open naturally in your hand.

Leaf

Roll a strip of quilling paper tightly around the quilling tool; then remove the circle from the tool. Pinch both ends of the circle.

Petal

Roll a strip of quilling paper tightly around the quilling tool; then remove the circle from the tool. Pinch one end of the circle.

 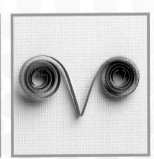

Scroll

Create an "S" shape by first rolling one end of the quilling paper toward you and then rolling the other end away from you.

V-scroll

Fold the quilling paper in half. Roll each end of the quilling paper away from the center.

Heart

Fold the quilling paper in half. Roll each end of the quilling paper toward the center.

Paper Pendant

Attach this charm to a necklace, bracelet, shoelace, or key chain.

Supplies

- quilling paper
- quilling tool
- liquid craft glue
- decoupage glue
- foam brush
- **Pendant** card stock

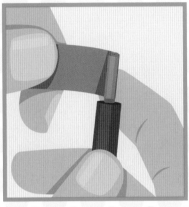

1. Insert a strip of quilling paper into the quilling tool and roll tightly. Remove it from the tool.

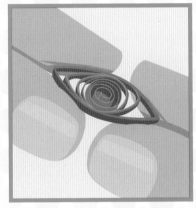

2. Pinch the quilled circle on both sides; then secure the shape by attaching the loose end with a dot of glue. Let dry. Repeat steps 1 and 2 seven more times.

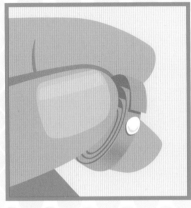

3. Roll one more quilling-paper strip in a contrasting color. Glue the circle closed.

Use one of these flower charms to decorate another craft in this book, such as the wallet on page 11 or the crown on page 52.

4. Spread a layer of decoupage glue on a pendant punch-out; arrange the quilled shapes on top. Let dry.

17

Rose Ring

A rose on the hand is better than two on the bush!

Supplies

- quilling paper
- quilling tool
- adhesive dots
- paper for ring
- scissors

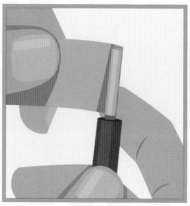

1. Insert a strip of quilling paper into the quilling tool slit. Hold the paper horizontally with your left hand; roll clockwise two turns with your right hand.

2. Fold the paper back and down to form an angle. Roll the paper gently over the fold, holding the strip out as you roll.

3. Keep holding the paper out, folding it back and down, and rolling over the folds until you reach the end of the strip.

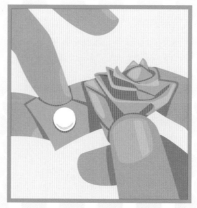

4. Remove the rose from the quilling tool. Secure the end of the paper with a small adhesive dot.

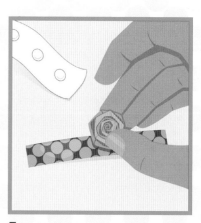

5. Cut a 2½-by-3/8-inch paper strip. Attach the rose bottom to the strip with an adhesive dot. Glue the ends together with a dot to form the ring.

Make a larger rose by cutting and curling a strip of paper that is 12 inches long and ½ inch wide.

Folded Bracelets

These origami-inspired bangles are made from nothing but paper!

Supplies

- **Bracelet** paper
- adhesive dots

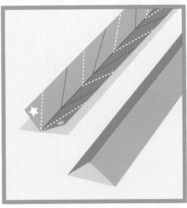

1. Separate bracelet paper into strips. Fold a strip lengthwise along the score, front sides together. Unfold and refold, back sides together. Unfold.

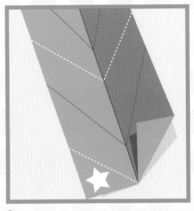

2. At the starred end, with stars facing up, fold the paper up along the first set of score lines (white) on each side of the center crease.

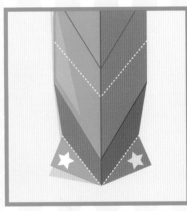

3. Fold down along the next set of score lines (black), to form a peak on each side of the center crease.

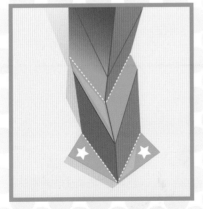

4. Fold up along the next set of score lines (white), forming a valley on each side of the center crease.

5. Continue folding, alternating peaks and valleys, to the end of the paper. The bracelet will curve and form a circle.

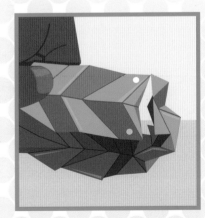

6. Overlap ends, lining up stars with dot marks. Place a small adhesive dot on each dot mark; secure. Pinch the sides of the bracelet for best fit.

Bedroom

Stop, wrap, and roll!
Transform your space with
paper perfection.

"Paperback" Books

Personalize hardcover books with this easy paper craft.

Supplies

- hardcover book
- paper
- pencil
- scissors
- tape

1. Trace around an open book on the back of the paper. Trim around the book, leaving 4 inches on all sides.

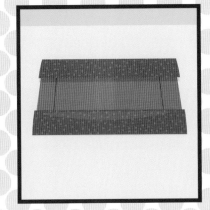

2. Fold in the top and bottom along the pencil lines.

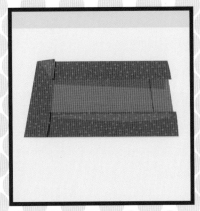

3. Fold in the left side along the pencil line.

Heavy-duty wrapping paper or oversized sheets of scrapbook paper work best for this project.

4. Make a pocket for the front cover by taping the inside of the left fold to the bottom and top folds. Slide in the front cover. Close the book with the front facedown on the work surface.

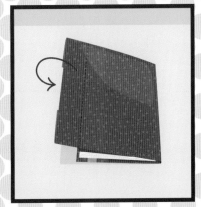

5. Fold the right side of the paper over the back cover. Prefold the paper over the edge of the back cover to mark the fold for the pocket.

6. Open the book cover. Make a back-cover pocket by taping the inside of the right fold to the bottom and top folds. Slide in the back cover.

Rolled Paper Frame

Make picture-perfect frames with patterned paper.

Supplies

- picture frame
- ruler
- **Picture Frame** paper
- scissors
- quilling tool
- liquid craft glue

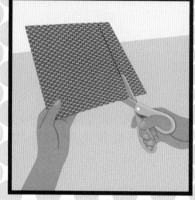

1. Measure the width of the sides surrounding the frame. Cut many strips of picture frame paper as wide as the frame sides and about 3 inches long.

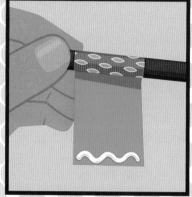

2. Roll paper tightly around the violet handle of the tool (not the quilling end). Secure the paper roll with a line of glue along its edge. Let dry. Repeat with all the strips.

3. Attach paper rolls to the frame with glue. Let dry.

An unfinished wood frame works best. For every inch around the frame, you'll need about 3 paper rolls.

Wrap and Roll Writing

Desktop tools look like pretty presents with this fun wrapping.

Supplies

- **Desktop Tools** paper
- new pencil
- scissors
- decoupage glue
- foam brush

1. Cut a strip of paper 1½ inches wide and as long as a new, unsharpened pencil.

2. Brush a thin layer of decoupage glue on the back of the paper, covering it completely.

3. Roll the pencil tightly onto the paper, starting at one edge. Secure it by pressing and holding. Let it dry overnight before sharpening the pencil.

> Make a matching pencil jar from a plastic or cardboard cylinder. Cut a strip of paper to wrap around the container, plus ¼ inch to overlap. Brush decoupage glue onto the paper and wrap it tightly.

Spiral Art

Paper twirls become a dizzying display of creativity.

Supplies

- picture frame
- card stock
- scissors
- quilling strips
- quilling tool
- liquid craft glue
- decoupage glue
- foam brush

1. Have an adult remove the glass from a deep frame; discard. Cut card stock to the same size as the removed glass; insert it into the frame. Turn the frame faceup.

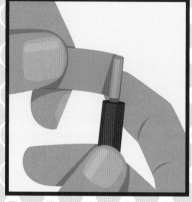

2. Roll quilling strips with the quilling tool to form coils. Secure each with a dot of glue as you work. Pinch into shapes, if desired.

3. Brush a thin layer of decoupage glue onto the front of the card stock.

4. Attach quilled shapes to the card stock. Let dry overnight.

Use any card stock or cardboard. See leaf, petal, heart, and scroll quilling shapes on page 15 for decorating ideas.

Leaf Wreath

Rolled paper leaves create a bright circle of color.

Supplies

- cardboard
- pencil
- scissors
- colored paper
- **Leaf Wreath** template card stock
- stapler

Find a sheet of cardboard in the back of any pad of scrapbook paper.

1. Using round lids or plates, trace one large circle onto cardboard. Trace a smaller circle inside the large circle.

2. Cut out the large circle. Fold it in half, and cut a slit in the center. Cut out the inner circle.

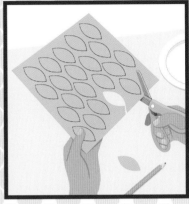

3. With the leaf wreath template, trace leaves onto different colors of paper and cut them out.

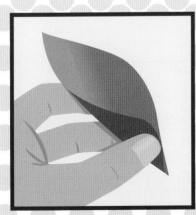

4. Roll the bottom point of each leaf into a cone shape, with sides slightly overlapping. Flatten with your finger.

5. Have an adult staple the flattened point to the cardboard circle.

6. Repeat steps 4 and 5 until the wreath is fully covered with overlapping leaves.

Signature Garland

Put your initials on display with this fan-filled banner.

Supplies

- **Signature Garland** card stock
- adhesive dots
- string
- **Signature Garland** circles card stock
- rhinestone letter stickers
- wide ribbon
- tape

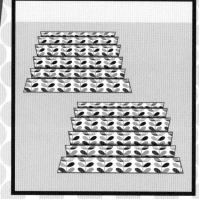

1. Separate each of the garland card-stock sheets in two. Accordion-fold rectangles from top to bottom on the score marks.

2. Fold each rectangle in half. Attach the halves together with adhesive dots.

3. Knot string tightly around the center. Fan out the paper. Connect the fans at the sides with adhesive dots. Repeat steps 2 and 3 for each fan.

4. Attach a garland circle to each fan center with an adhesive dot. Finish each with a rhinestone letter sticker.

5. Attach a wide ribbon to the backs of the fans with small strips of tape at the fan tops and bottoms.

Personalize your desk chair, headboard, or window with your initials, short words, or numbers such as a special date.

Paper Chandelier

Dangling disks create a mesmerizing mobile.

Supplies

- **Chandelier** circles card stock
- thread
- jumbo craft sticks
- adhesive dot
- tape
- ribbon

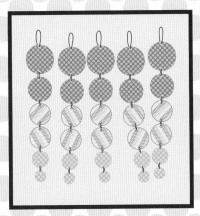

1. Punch out card-stock chandelier circles. Punch out the holes in the circles. Create 5 long chains by attaching circles together with individual pieces of thread.

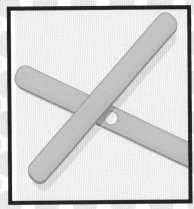

2. Create a cross shape with two craft sticks. Secure it with an adhesive dot.

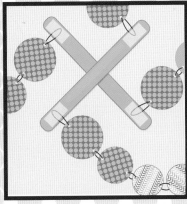

3. With tape, secure the top of a chain to each of the stick ends and to the center cross point.

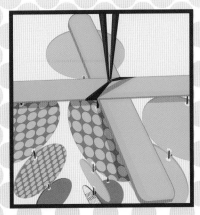

4. Knot ribbon around the center of the craft sticks to hang.

> For extra color, connect the circles with contrasting quilling paper, like the chandelier pictured here.

Folded Flowers

Spectacular petals blossom into a tabletop garden.

Supplies

- 5 paper squares
- adhesive dots
- liquid craft glue
- paper clips

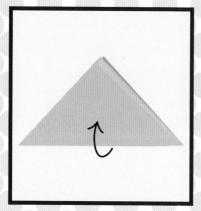

1. Rotate a square piece of paper into a diamond shape. Fold the bottom half up.

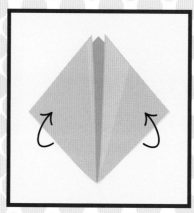

2. Fold the left and right points in toward the top center point to form a diamond shape.

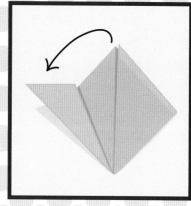

3. Fold the top left point in half diagonally toward the left side. Fold the top right point in half diagonally toward the right side.

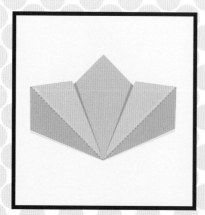

4. Unfold each side. Pop folded portions open; then press along the fold in each side to flatten into kite shapes, as pictured.

For each flower, you'll need 5 pieces of square paper—one for each petal. For larger flowers, use larger paper. Just make sure all 5 sheets are the same size. Also, your paper needs to be colored or decorated on both front and back.

Instructions continue on the next page.

Folded Flowers

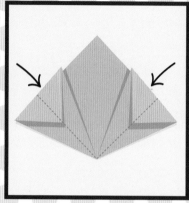

5. Fold the top point of each kite shape down toward you.

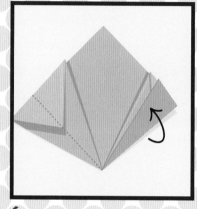

6. Fold the kite shapes in half toward the center point.

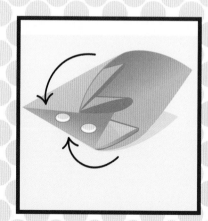

7. Attach the folded corners together with adhesive dots to create a cone shape. Repeat all steps 4 more times to create a total of 5 petals.

8. Line the outside edges of the petals with glue. Secure petals together with paper clips to form the flower. Let dry. Remove paper clips.

Make flowers in different sizes for a beautiful bouquet. Use 12-by-12-inch paper or larger for the most magnificent blooms.

Add stems to your flowers with adhesive dots and lollipop sticks.

Party

Paper sets the stage for celebration— just add friends!

Paper Rose Streamers

This garland looks like a blossoming bouquet—no water required!

Supplies

- **Rose Streamer** card stock
- adhesive dots
- wide ribbon

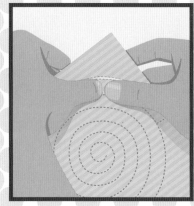

1. Separate rose streamer card stock into 20 squares. For each square, punch out along the perforated line to create a spiral.

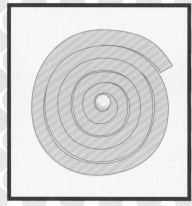

2. Place an adhesive dot in the middle of the center tab.

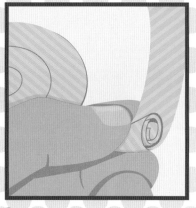

3. Starting at the outside edge of the spiral, roll the paper tightly between your fingers. Continue rolling to the center tab.

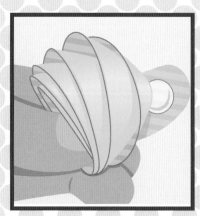

4. Press the rose firmly onto the adhesive dot on the center tab, keeping the coils of the rose in place until secure.

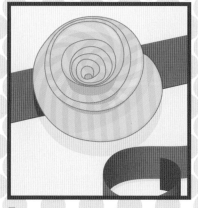

5. Attach an adhesive dot to the ribbon; press the rose onto it. Repeat steps 1–5, adding roses to the ribbon streamer.

Adjust the size of the rose by letting the coil loosen between your fingers. Create smaller roses by cutting off part of the spiral before rolling.

Ombré Paper Chains

Create a colorful backdrop that's reminiscent of a rainbow.

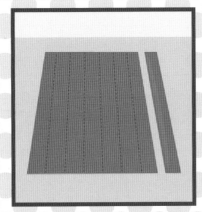

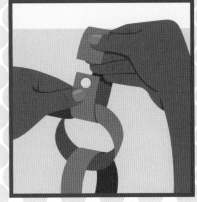

1. Separate the ombré chain paper into strips along the perforated lines.

2. Start with one strip. Secure the ends together with an adhesive dot to create a loop.

3. Insert a second strip through the first loop. Secure the ends together with an adhesive dot to create a second loop. Repeat until the chain is as long as you like.

Ombré (ohm-bray) is a term used to describe colors that fade from one into another or a color that shifts gradually from light to dark. To make your chain look ombré, transition from shades of pink to shades of orange or from shades of blue to shades of green.

Paper Crown

Party guests will love to tie on one of these happy hats.

Supplies

- **Crown** card stock
- ruler
- scissors
- hole punch
- thin ribbon

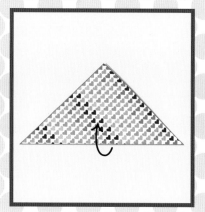

1. Fold the crown card stock in half diagonally. Measure up 4 inches from the fold, and cut off the top triangle.

2. Make zigzag cuts along the edge opposite the fold.

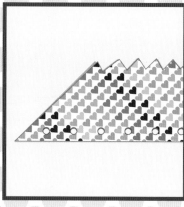

3. Punch holes, spaced 1½ inches apart, about ½ inch above the fold.

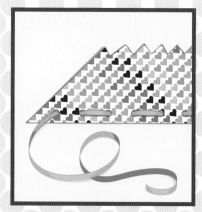

4. Weave ribbon through the holes. Place the crown on your head. Tie the ribbon in a bow at the back of the crown.

Use different colors and patterns of heavy-weight scrapbook paper to make crowns for everyone at the party!

Treat Toppers

Petite pinwheels make cupcakes even sweeter.

Supplies

- **Treat Topper** paper
- ruler
- pencil
- scissors
- adhesive dots
- **Treat Topper** circles paper
- lollipop sticks
- tape

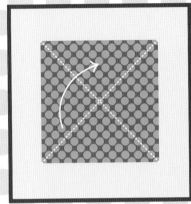

1. Separate treat topper paper into nine squares along perforated lines. Fold each square in half diagonally, unfold, and then fold diagonally in the other direction.

2. Unfold the square completely. Use a pencil to mark ½ inch from the center point on each fold. Cut along all four folds to the pencil marks.

3. Place an adhesive dot on the right corner of each triangle shape. Fold the corners into the center. Without creasing the folds, press to secure the adhesive dots.

4. Attach a treat topper circle at the center with an adhesive dot.

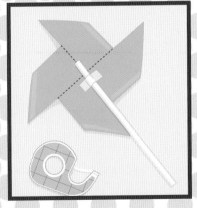

5. Tape a 4-inch lollipop stick to the back of the pinwheel.

Make a large adhesive dot smaller by cutting it in half while it's still on the wrapper.

Paper Poufs

These pretty poufs float like fluffy clouds above your party.

Supplies

- tissue paper
- ribbon or string
- scissors

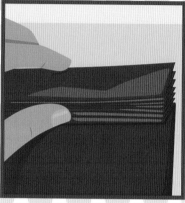

1. Stack 10 sheets of tissue paper. Accordion-fold the stack. Tie a long ribbon or string around the center.

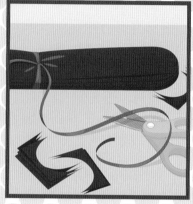

2. Trim both ends of the stack so that they are rounded instead of square.

3. Gently pull each sheet of tissue paper up and toward the center.

4. Hang the pouf from the ribbon.

Make smaller or bigger poufs by altering the size of the original square. Or stack tissue paper of different shades of colors to make ombré poufs!

Origami Box

Who needs a goody bag when you can make a goody box?

Supplies

- **Origami Box**
  paper

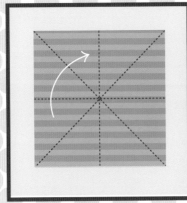

1. Fold and unfold the box paper diagonally both ways. Fold it in half both left to right and top to bottom. Unfold it completely.

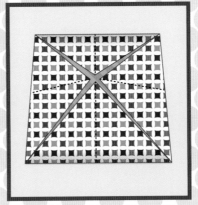

2. Rotate paper 1/8 turn. Fold each corner into the center.

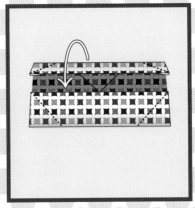

3. Fold the bottom up to the center line and the top down to the center.

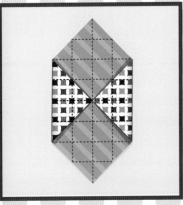

4. Unfold the top and bottom halves completely.

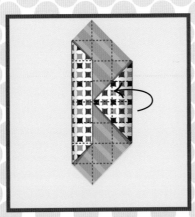

5. Fold the left and right sides into the center. Unfold halves slightly so that the triangles stay on the box bottom and left and right sides stand up.

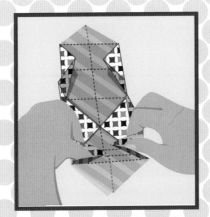

6. With left and right sides up, fold in at the box's bottom corners and fold the bottom triangle up, over corner folds, and in toward the center.

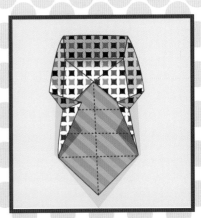

7. Adjust paper along the creases to form a third side, with a triangle flat on the box bottom. Rotate the box; repeat steps 6–7 to form the final side.

Fringed Gift Wrap

Nothing says "party" like streamers and presents!

Supplies

- crepe paper streamers
- gift bag
- ruler
- scissors
- glue stick

1. Cut strips of streamers as long as a gift bag's width.

2. Stack streamers. Snip slits 1 inch deep along their length.

3. Starting at the bottom of the gift bag, draw a line of glue across the bag with a glue stick. Attach the streamer.

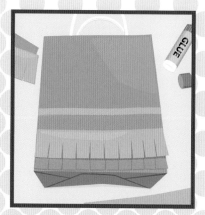

4. Draw another line of glue 1 inch above the first layer so that the next streamer will overlap. Attach the next streamer. Repeat until the gift bag is covered.

Decorate a box or a bag with this fringed front, and fluff the fringe for a fun finish!

Here are some other American Girl books you might like:

Discover online games, quizzes, activities,
and more at **americangirl.com/play**